An Expert Navajo Weaver

by Luisa Birchwood

Harcourt
SCHOOL PUBLISHERS

Cover, ©Pete Saloutos/CORBIS; p.3, ©Carl & Ann Purcell/CORBIS; p.4-5, p.7, p.9, ©Paul Conklin/ PhotoEdit; p.6, p.10, ©Catherine Karnow/CORBIS; p.8, ©Deborah Davis/PhotoEdit; p.11, ©ARPL/ Topham/The Image Works; p.12, ©Christie's Images/CORBIS; p.13, ©Lowe Art Museum/SuperStock; p.14, ©Mark Gibson/Index Stock.

Copyright © by Harcourt, Inc.

All rights reserved. No part of this publication may be reproduced or transmitted in any form or by any means, electronic or mechanical, including photocopy, recording, or any information storage and retrieval system, without permission in writing from the publisher.

Requests for permission to make copies of any part of the work should be addressed to School Permissions and Copyrights, Harcourt, Inc., 6277 Sea Harbor Drive, Orlando, Florida 32887-6777. Fax: 407-345-2418.

HARCOURT and the Harcourt Logo are trademarks of Harcourt, Inc., registered in the United States of America and/or other jurisdictions.

Printed in China

ISBN 10: 0-15-351524-4
ISBN 13: 978-0-15-351524-8

Ordering Options
ISBN 10: 0-15-351214-8 (Grade 4 Advanced Collection)
ISBN 13: 978-0-15-351214-8 (Grade 4 Advanced Collection)
ISBN 10: 0-15-358114-X (package of 5)
ISBN 13: 978-0-15-358114-4 (package of 5)

If you have received these materials as examination copies free of charge, Harcourt School Publishers retains title to the materials and they may not be resold. Resale of examination copies is strictly prohibited and is illegal.

Possession of this publication in print format does not entitle users to convert this publication, or any portion of it, into electronic format.

4 5 6 7 8 9 10 0940 12 11 10 09

Marilou Schultz is a Navajo weaver. She knows all about Navajo rugs and blankets. That's because she's been around them her whole life. Her mother was a Navajo weaver. So was her grandmother. Her great-grandmother was, too. Even her *great-great-grandmother* was a Navajo weaver! "Weaving has always been part of my life," Marilou said.

Marilou became inspired to make her own Navajo weavings. She began to do so while just a child. Today she is an expert weaver. She weaves beautiful Navajo blankets and rugs, and she teaches others how to weave. She carries on the Navajo weaving tradition.

Marilou was born in Safford, Arizona, in 1954. She grew up in Leupp, Arizona, which is on the Navajo reservation. Marilou remembers being woken up once as a child by the sounds of her mother weaving.

Marilou learned to weave by watching her mother. Marilou became more and more skilled over time. She was already weaving complete Navajo rugs when she was in elementary school. She was even able to sell the rugs to earn money. As she grew older, she continued to make and sell weavings. This allowed her to support herself.

Today Marilou's family weaving tradition continues. Her son weaves, as do her nieces and nephews. In fact, her niece Krystal Schultz won an award for her Navajo weaving.

"Navajo weaving has always been and continues to be passed on in my family," Marilou said.

The Navajo have been making blankets for a long time. At first, the Navajo people lived in Canada. About 1,000 years ago, a group of Navajo settled in the southwestern area of what is now the United States. They became farmers.

The Pueblo people lived in that region. They knew how to weave and make cloth. They used cotton and grasses to weave blankets. The Pueblo taught the Navajo how to weave and build looms. Looms are simple machines used for weaving.

Several hundred years later, Spanish people came and brought sheep with them from Spain. The hair that grows on sheep is called wool. The Navajo learned how to weave blankets from wool.

A student weaver

Getting the wool is the first step in making a Navajo blanket. The traditional Navajo way to do this was to let the wool grow on the sheep. The Navajo waited until the wool was long and thick. They had to pay close attention to the wool because sometimes it would become infested with insects. Once the wool was long, they would delicately shear the sheep. To *shear* means "to cut off the wool."

Next, the Navajo cleaned the wool. First, they shook it to remove any twigs, and then it was washed. This would get rid of most of the oil on the wool. Then the Navajo would let the wool dry in the sun. This made the wool fluffy. Finally, the wool was "carded" to untangle it. Carding is similar to combing.

A weaver spinning yarn

Marilou usually buys yarn for her own weaving. Sometimes for special projects, though, she actually starts with wool and spins it into yarn, just like her ancestors did. She spins the wool using a spindle. The spindle is a stick that has a wooden circle on the end of it. Marilou wraps some wool around the spindle. Then she rolls the circle on her leg, which stretches and twists the wool into thin strands. Sometimes Marilou will spin the yarn three or four times.

Next, Marilou dyes the yarn so that her blanket will have color. Like her Navajo ancestors, she may use natural herbs, roots, or vegetables to make the dyes. Her ancestors would grind up things such as grapes, prickly pear cactus, or thistle, and then add water to them to form a dye. Then the yarn was dipped into the dye. This bonded the color to the yarn.

    The actual weaving of the blanket takes place on a loom. Navajo weavers work on vertical looms. This means that the loom stands upright, unlike horizontal looms, which lie flat on the ground. To set up the Navajo loom, two thin pieces of wood are planted into the ground about five or six feet apart. A thin branch is then hung across the top. The yarn is hung from this thin branch so that the blanket hangs in front of the weaver.

Marilou first hangs long pieces of yarn from the top of the loom. These stretch all the way to the bottom of the loom. She keeps adding the pieces of yarn until there is yarn hanging all the way across the top of the loom. She then attaches these pieces to the bottom part of the loom to hold them in place. These pieces of yarn that run vertically, or up and down, are called the *warp*.

Marilou takes out a thin piece of wood called a *batten*. The batten is like a long ruler. She carefully passes the batten through the warp yarn. She first passes it *over* one piece of yarn, then *under* the next piece of yarn, then *over* the following piece of yarn, and so on.

weaver at a loom

Now the batten is in place. This allows the weaver to pass yarn easily through the warp threads. She takes a piece of the yarn and begins to pass it through the warp threads. Because of the batten, the thread goes over one thread, underneath the next, and so on. These pieces of thread that pass through horizontally, or side to side, are called the *weft*. The batten creates an opening in the warp threads, and the weft threads pass through this opening.

The weft threads, or yarn, give the blanket colors or patterns. If the weaver wants black running horizontally across her blanket, she'll use black thread. She will run this black weft thread through the warp threads and then tap it down with a weaving fork. Because the work is so detailed, weavers often work in short intervals.

This is a newly-woven Navajo blanket. It has been made to look just like the early Navajo weavings. Most of the early Navajo blankets were striped. In fact, when young Navajo women first learned to weave, their first project was usually to make a simple striped blanket.

The threads for these early blankets were colored with natural dyes, so they were not very colorful. The blankets were usually white with black, brown, or gray stripes. In the early 1800s, though, the Navajo began to purchase clothing or blankets that came from Spain and were made of red cloth. The Navajo unraveled the clothing or blankets to get the red thread. Then they used the thread in their weavings. As a result, the Navajo weavings became more colorful.

This is called a Chief Blanket. As the Navajo became better weavers, they began to make Chief Blankets. Chief blankets have much thicker stripes. Most of them have wide white, black, and red stripes. Later Navajo weavers began to add diamonds to their Chief Blankets. Over the years, the diamonds became larger and larger.

They became known as "Chief Blankets" because they were often given to Native American leaders, as well as to American military leaders. Many people wanted to have one of these beautiful, but very expensive, blankets.

Sometimes the Navajo weavers would cut a slit in the center of a Chief Blanket. This made the blanket more flexible in its use because people could place their heads through the hole and wear the weaving like a poncho.

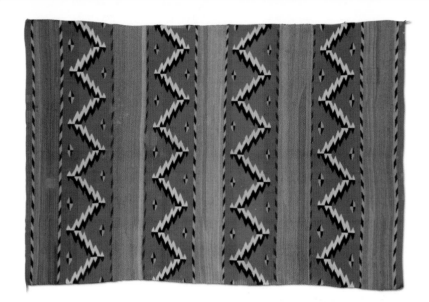

This type of Navajo weaving is called an "Eye-Dazzler" because it "dazzles the eye" with colors and unique patterns. The Navajo began to make blankets like these in the 1880s. It was at that time that the Navajo began to buy wool from a mill in Pennsylvania. This wool was bright and colorful, so the Navajo weavers began to make blankets that had brilliant reds, blues, and yellows in them. The weavers also started to make more complicated patterns.

The Navajo sold many of their weavings to trading posts. In order to sell more of their weavings, the Navajo began to make them thicker and heavier. People bought these heavier weavings and used them as wall hangings or rugs instead of using them as blankets.

Marilou is proud to help preserve the Navajo way of weaving. "The techniques I use are the traditional ways of weaving Navajo rugs, and this sets them apart from other weaving traditions," she said.

Marilou displays and sells her weavings at the Heard Museum Indian Fair and Market. This event is held each year in Phoenix, Arizona. She has won awards at the fair for her weavings four times! She also attends the Santa Fe Indian Market. Hundreds of artists from many different American Indian groups come to this market to show their works. Marilou has shown her weavings there for over twenty years.

"I weave because of my love of weaving and the challenge of creating unique weavings," Marilou once said. Given her family history, she will likely weave for many more years. After all, her grandmother wove until she was in her mid–90s!

Think Critically

1. What does the author think about Navajo weavings?

2. How did the traditional Navajo people get the wool they needed for their weavings?

3. What is a word that means almost the same thing as *unique* does on page 13?

4. What is one opinion stated in this story?

5. What are some details from this story that interested you? Why?

 Art

Draw and Color a Chief Blanket Look back at some of the blanket designs in this book. Draw an outline of a blanket. Then design your own blanket in the Navajo style. Color it with markers or colored pencils.

School-Home Connection Tell a family member about how the traditional Navajo people got the wool for their weavings. Then have a discussion about why people might want to preserve old traditions.

Word Count: 1,517 (1,529)